Salisbury Vespers

Bob Chilcott

for chorus, chamber choir, and children's choir, or large divisi chorus, with orchestra or brass ensemble and organ

Vocal score

MUSIC DEPARTMENT

OXFORD
UNIVERSITY PRESS

T0056081

OXFORD

UNIVERSITY PRESS

Great Clarendon Street, Oxford OX2 6DP, England
198 Madison Avenue, New York, NY 10016, USA

Oxford University Press is a department of the University of Oxford.
It furthers the University's aim of excellence in research, scholarship,
and education by publishing worldwide in

Oxford New York

Auckland Bangkok Buenos Aires Cape Town Chennai
Dar es Salaam Delhi Hong Kong Istanbul Karachi Kolkata
Kuala Lumpur Madrid Melbourne Mexico City Mumbai Nairobi
São Paulo Shanghai Taipei Tokyo Toronto

1 3 5 7 9 10 8 6 4 2

ISBN 978-0-19-336395-3

Music and text origination by
Enigma Music Production Services, Amersham, Bucks.
Printed in Great Britain on acid-free paper by
Halstan & Co. Ltd., Amersham, Bucks.

Contents

Scoring

Salisbury Vespers is scored for chorus, chamber choir, and children's choir, but can equally be performed by a large mixed chorus divided into smaller groups, with sopranos and altos singing the children's part.

TUTTI CHOIRS indicates that all three choirs should sing, with members of the children's choir singing the soprano or alto lines as desired. When a section for **TUTTI CHOIRS** is divided into parts for two separate choirs, singers should divide within each choir unless otherwise indicated in the score.

A separate part for the children's choir is also available (ISBN 978-0-19-336464-6).

Instrumentation

The accompaniment to this work exists in two versions:

1. For full orchestra

2 flutes
2 oboes
2 clarinets in B flat
2 bassoons
4 horns in F
3 trumpets in B flat
2 trombones
bass trombone
tuba
timpani
percussion 1 (side drum, tubular bells, medium and low tom-toms, triangle, crash cymbals)
percussion 2 (bass drum, glockenspiel, crotales, bongos)
organ (optional)
strings

2. For brass ensemble and organ

2 horns in F
4 trumpets in B flat
2 trombones
bass trombone
tuba
timpani
percussion 1 and 2 (as above)
organ

The piano accompaniment printed in this score is an orchestral reduction for rehearsal purposes only.

Full scores and instrumental parts for the orchestral accompaniment are available on hire from the publisher; material for brass ensemble and organ will be available on hire from October 2009.

Composer's note

Salisbury Vespers was first performed in May 2009 in the magnificent medieval cathedral in Salisbury, an event that involved five hundred singers from seven different choirs based in the city. The piece was designed in such a way that the choirs could be situated in different parts of this huge building and could therefore use the complete space to surround the audience with sound. The challenge this presented musically dictated the way that several of the sections have been put together, but it was always my intention that this work would function just as well within the normal set-up of a performance space. The work is designed to involve a large mixed choir, a chamber choir, and a children's choir, but could equally be performed by a large mixed choir, with the chamber choir and children's choir parts being sung by smaller sections taken from within the large choir.

Salisbury Vespers is a concert work based on the ancient evening service of Vespers. After the opening antiphon, three psalm settings and a setting of the great Passiontide hymn 'Vexilla Regis prodeunt' are interspersed by four motets on Marian texts, reflecting the dedication of Salisbury Cathedral to the Blessed Virgin Mary. The first is a Christmas text and the second tells of the Presentation of Jesus at the Temple; the third is a text from the Passion, while the fourth, taken from the Sarum Rite, is in praise of the Virgin Mary. The work ends with a setting of the Magnificat, based, as in the great setting of 1610 by Claudio Monteverdi, on the plainsong melody Tone 1.

I am grateful to all the singers and players from Salisbury for their commitment and dedication to this project, and particularly to those who have led it, notably Fiona Clarke, John Powell, John Elliott, and David Halls. For their work on this publication I would like to thank Mary Chandler and Ralph Woodward, and Robyn Carpenter for her careful and supportive editorial work.

Duration: *c*.50 minutes

Salisbury Vespers was commissioned by the following musical organizations in Salisbury, England:

Salisbury Community Choir
Salisbury Musical Society
Salisbury Symphony Orchestra
Sarum Voices
St John Singers
The Farrant Singers

The first performance of *Salisbury Vespers* was given in Salisbury Cathedral on 23 May 2009, in association with the Salisbury International Arts Festival, by the choirs and orchestra named, and with the Salisbury Cathedral Choir and Salisbury Cathedral Junior Choir, conducted by David Halls, Director of Music, Salisbury Cathedral.

This project has been generously supported by 'Specsavers' Salisbury.

Texts and translations

These texts and translations may be reproduced as required for programme notes.

1. Psalm 69 (70): Deus in adiutorium

Deus in adiutorium meum intende.
Domine ad adiuvandum me festina.
Gloria Patri et Filio et Spiritui Sancto:
Sicut erat in principio, et nunc et semper, et in saecula saeculorum. Amen.
Alleluia.

O God, come to our aid.
O Lord, make haste to help us.
Glory be to the Father, and to the Son: and to the Holy Ghost;
As it was in the beginning, is now, and ever shall be: world without end. Amen.
Alleluia.

2. Psalm 109 (110): Dixit Dominus

Dixit Dominus Domino meo: sede a dextris meis: donec ponam inimicos tuos scabellum pedum tuorum.
Virgam virtutis tuae emittet Dominus ex Sion: dominare in medio inimicorum tuorum.
Tecum principium in die virtutis tuae in splendoribus sanctorum: ex utero ante luciferum genui te.
Iuravit Dominus, et non paenitebit eum: tu es sacerdos in aeternum secundum ordinem Melchisedech.
Dominus a dextris tuis, confregit in die irae suae reges.
Iudicabit in nationibus, implebit ruinas: conquassabit capita in terra multorum.
De torrente in via bibet: propterea exaltabit caput.
Gloria Patri et Filio et Spiritui Sancto:
Sicut erat in principio, et nunc et semper, et in saecula saeculorum. Amen.

The Lord said unto my Lord: Sit thou on my right hand, until I make thine enemies thy footstool.
The Lord shall send the rod of thy power out of Sion: be thou ruler, even in the midst among thine enemies.
In the day of thy power shall the people offer thee free-will offerings with an holy worship: the dew of thy birth is of the womb of the morning.
The Lord sware, and will not repent: Thou art a priest for ever after the order of Melchisedech.
The Lord upon thy right hand: shall wound even kings in the day of his wrath.
He shall judge among the heathen; he shall fill the places with the dead bodies: and smite in sunder the heads over divers countries.
He shall drink of the brook in the way: therefore shall he lift up his head.
Glory be to the Father, and to the Son: and to the Holy Ghost;
As it was in the beginning, is now, and ever shall be: world without end. Amen.

3. I sing of a mayden

Anon. 15th century

I sing of a mayden
That is makèles:[1]
King of all Kings
To her son she ches.[2]

He came also stille
To his moder's[3] bour,[4]
As dew in Aprille
That falleth on the flour.[5]

He came also stille
There his moder lay,
As dew in Aprille
That falleth on the spray.

Moder and mayden
Was never none but she:
Well may such a lady
Goddes[6] moder be.

[1] makèles = matchless
[2] ches = chose
[3] moder = mother

[4] bour = bower (womb)
[5] flour = flower
[6] Goddes = God's

4. Psalm 112 (113): Laudate pueri

Laudate pueri Dominum: laudate nomen Domini.
Sit nomen Domini benedictum, ex hoc nunc, et usque in saeculum.
A solis ortu usque ad occasum: laudabile nomen Domini.
Excelsus super omnes gentes Dominus: et super coelos gloria eius.
Quis sicut Dominus Deus noster, qui in altis habitat: et humilia respicit in caelo et in terra?
Suscitans a terra inopem: et de stercore erigens pauperem:
ut collocet eum cum principibus, cum principibus populi sui.
Qui habitare facit sterilem in domo, matrem filiorum laetantem.
Gloria Patri et Filio et Spiritui Sancto:
Sicut erat in principio, et nunc et semper, et in saecula saeculorum. Amen.

Praise the Lord, ye servants: O praise the Name of the Lord.
Blessed be the Name of the Lord: from this time forth for evermore.
The Lord's Name is praise: from the rising up of the sun unto the going down of the same.
The Lord is high above all heathen: and his glory above the heavens.
Who is like unto the Lord our God, that hath his dwelling so high: and yet humbleth himself
to behold the things that are in heaven and earth?
He taketh up the simple out of the dust: and lifteth the poor out of the mire;
That he may set him with the princes: even with the princes of his people.
He maketh the barren woman to keep house: and to be a joyful mother of children.
Glory be to the Father, and to the Son: and to the Holy Ghost;
As it was in the beginning, is now, and ever shall be: world without end. Amen.

5. When to the temple Mary went

Johannes Eccard (1553–1611), trans. Revd John Troutbeck (1832–99)

When to the temple Mary went,
And brought the Holy Child,
Him did the aged Simeon see,
As it had been revealed.

He took up Jesus in his arms
And, blessing God, he said:
'In peace I now depart
My Saviour having seen,
The hope of Israel,
The light of men.'

Help now thy servants, gracious Lord,
That we may ever be,
As once the faithful Simeon was,
Rejoicing but in thee:
And when we must from Earth departure take,
May we gently fall asleep,
And with thee awake.

6. Psalm 121 (122): Laetatus sum

Laetatus sum in his quae dicta sunt mihi: in domum Domini ibimus.
Stantes erant pedes nostri in atriis tuis, Jerusalem.
Jerusalem, quae aedificatur ut civitas: cuius participatio eius in idipsum.
Illuc enim ascenderunt tribus, tribus Domini: testimonium Israel ad confitendum nomini Domini.
Quia illic sederunt sedes in iudicio, sedes super domum David.
Rogate quae ad pacem sunt Jerusalem: et abundantia diligentibus te.
Fiat pax in virtute tua: et abundantia in turribus tuis.
Propter fratres meos et proximos meos, loquebar pacem de te;
Propter domum Domini Dei nostri, quaesivi bona tibi.
Gloria Patri et Filio et Spiritui Sancto:
Sicut erat in principio, et nunc et semper, et in saecula saeculorum. Amen.

I was glad when they said unto me: We will go into the house of the Lord.
Our feet shall stand in thy gates: O Jerusalem.
Jerusalem is built as a city: that is at unity in itself.
For thither the tribes go up, even the tribes of the Lord: to testify unto Israel, to give thanks unto the Name of the Lord.
For there is the seat of judgement: even the seat of the house of David.
O pray for the peace of Jerusalem: they shall prosper that love thee.
Peace be within thy walls: and plenteousness within thy palaces.
For my brethren and companions' sakes: I will wish thee prosperity.
Yea, because of the house of the Lord our God: I will seek to do thee good.
Glory be to the Father, and to the Son: and to the Holy Ghost;
As it was in the beginning, is now, and ever shall be: world without end. Amen.

7. Lovely tear of lovely eye

Anon. 14th century

Lovely tear of lovely eye,
Why dost thou me so woe?
Sorrowful tear of sorrowful eye,
Thou breakest my heart in two.

Thou grievest sore,
Thou sorrow is more
Than mankind's mouth may tell;
Thou singst of sorrow,
Mankind to borrow,
Out of the pit of hell.

Thy mother sees
What woe is to thee,
And earnestly cries out;
To her thou speak,
Her sorrow to ease;
Sweet pleading won thy heart.

Thou heart is rent,
Thy body bent
Upon the rood tree;
The weather is passed,
The devil defeated,
Christ, through the might of thee.

8. Hymn: Vexilla Regis prodeunt

Venantius Fortunatus (530–609)
Stanzas 1, 3–6, and 8–9 trans. J. M. Neale (1818–66); stanzas 2 and 7 trans. Leofranc Holford-Strevens

Vexilla Regis prodeunt;
fulget crucis mysterium,
quo carne carnis conditor
suspensus est patibulo.

The royal banners forward go,
the cross shines forth in mystic glow;
where he in flesh, our flesh who made,
our sentence bore, our ransom paid.

Confixa clavis viscera
tendens manus vestigia,
redemptionis gratia
hic immolata est hostia.

Sharp nails were through his body sped,
Outstretched his hands, his feet outspread;
That our redemption we might gain,
Our Lord in sacrifice was slain.

Quo vulneratus insuper
mucrone diro lanceae,
ut nos lavaret crimine,
manavit unda et sanguine.

Where deep for us the spear was dyed,
life's torrent rushing from his side,
to wash us in that precious flood,
where mingled water flowed, and blood.

Impleta sunt quae concinit
David fideli carmine,
dicendo nationibus:
regnavit a ligno Deus.

Arbor decora et fulgida,
ornata Regis purpura,
electa digno stipite
tam sancta membra tangere.

Beata, cuius brachiis
pretium pependit saeculi:
statera facta corporis,
praedam tulitque tartari.

Salve, ara, salve, victima,
de passionis gloria,
qua vita mortem pertulit
et morte vitam reddidit.

O crux ave, spes unica,
hoc Passionis tempore!
piis adauge gratiam
reisque dele crimina.

Te, fons salutis, Trinitas,
collaudet omnis spiritus;
quos per crucis mysterium
salvas fove per saecula. Amen.

Fulfilled is all that David told
in true prophetic song of old,
amidst the nations, God, saith he,
hath reigned and triumphed from the tree.

O tree of beauty, tree of light!
O tree with royal purple dight!
Elect on whose triumphal breast
those holy limbs should find their rest.

Upon its arms, like balance true,
he weighed the price for sinners due,
the price which none but he could pay,
and spoiled the spoiler of his prey.

Hail altar, hail the victim-king,
In whose all-glorious suffering
He that is Life to die yet bore
And dying did our life restore.

O cross, our one reliance, hail!
Still may thy power with us avail
to give new virtue to the saint,
and pardon to the penitent.

To thee, eternal Three in One,
let homage meet by all be done:
whom by the cross thou dost restore,
preserve and govern evermore. Amen.

9. Hail, Star of the sea most radiant

Sarum Primer, 1516

Hail, Star of the sea most radiant,
O mother of God most glorious,
A pure virgin always persevering.

O gate of heaven most gorgeous,
Thou was saluted with great humility
When Gabriel said, Ave Maria,
Establish us in peace and tranquillity,
And change the name of sinful Eve.

Loose the prisoners from captivity.
Unto the blind give sight again.
Deliver us from our malignity
To the end we may some grace attain.

10. Magnificat

Luke 1: 46–55

Magnificat anima mea Dominum.
Et exultavit spiritus meus in Deo salutari meo.
Quia respexit humilitatem ancillae suae: ecce enim ex hoc beatam me dicent omnes generationes.
Quia fecit mihi magna qui potens est: et sanctum nomen eius.
Et misericordia eius a progenie in progenies: timentibus eum.
Fecit potentiam in brachio suo: dispersit superbos mente cordis sui.
Deposuit potentes de sede: et exaltavit humiles.
Esurientes implevit bonis: et divites dimisit inanes,
Suscepit Israel puerum suum: recordatus misericordiae suae.
Sicut locutus est ad patres nostros: Abraham et semini eius in saecula.
Gloria Patri et Filio et Spiritui Sancto:
Sicut erat in principio, et nunc et semper, et in saecula saeculorum. Amen.

My soul doth magnify the Lord.
And my spirit hath rejoiced in God my Saviour.
For he hath regarded the lowliness of his handmaiden: for behold, from henceforth all generations shall call me blessed.
For he that is mighty hath magnified me: and holy is his Name.
And his mercy is on them that fear him: throughout all generations.
He hath showed strength with his arm: he hath scattered the proud in the imagination of their hearts.
He hath put down the mighty from their seat: and hath exalted the humble and meek.
He hath filled the hungry with good things: and the rich he hath sent empty away.
He remembering his mercy hath holpen his servant Israel: as he promised to our forefathers, Abraham and his seed, for ever.
Glory be to the Father, and to the Son: and to the Holy Ghost;
As it was in the beginning, is now, and ever shall be: world without end. Amen.

Salisbury Vespers

SALISBURY VESPERS

BOB CHILCOTT

1. Psalm 69 (70), v. 2: Deus in adiutorium

Printed in Great Britain

OXFORD UNIVERSITY PRESS, MUSIC DEPARTMENT, GREAT CLARENDON STREET, OXFORD OX2 6DP

Glo-ri-a Pa-tri et Fi-li-o et Spi-ri-tu-i Sanc-to:

Si-cut e-rat in prin-ci-pi-o, et nunc et sem-per,

sem-per, et in sae-cu-la sae-cu-lo-rum. A-men.

Al-le-lu-ia, al-le-lu - ia,   al-le-lu-ia, al-le - lu - ia, al-le - lu - ia.

2. *Psalm 109 (110): Dixit Dominus*

Di - xit Do - mi-nus,   di - xit Do-mi-nus,   di - xit Do - mi-nus,

Di - xit Do - mi - nus,   di - xit Do - mi - nus,   di - xit Do - mi -

3. Motet: *I sing of a mayden*

Anon. 15th century

[1] *ma-kè-les* = matchless
[2] *ches* = chose

[3] mo-der = mother

20

⁴*bour* = bower (womb)
⁵*flour* = flower

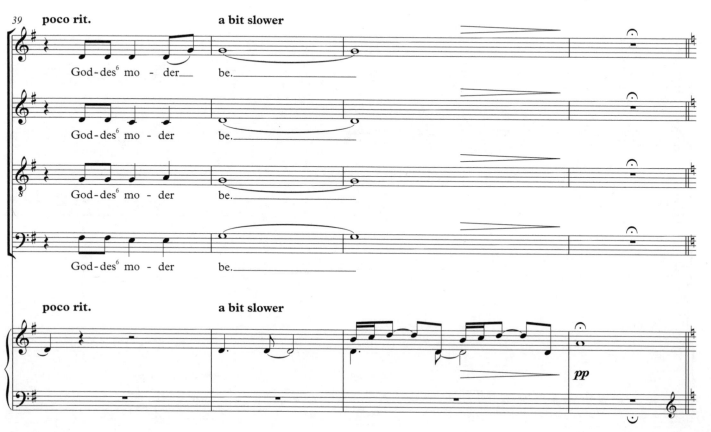

[6]*God-des* = God's

4. *Psalm 112 (113): Laudate pueri*

et su-per coe-los glo-ri-a, et su-per coe-los glo-ri-a e-ius.

Quis si-cut Do-mi-nus De-us nos-ter, qui in

al - tis ha-bi-tat: et hu-mi-li-a re-spi-cit in

coe - lo, in coe - lo et in ter - ra?

rit.

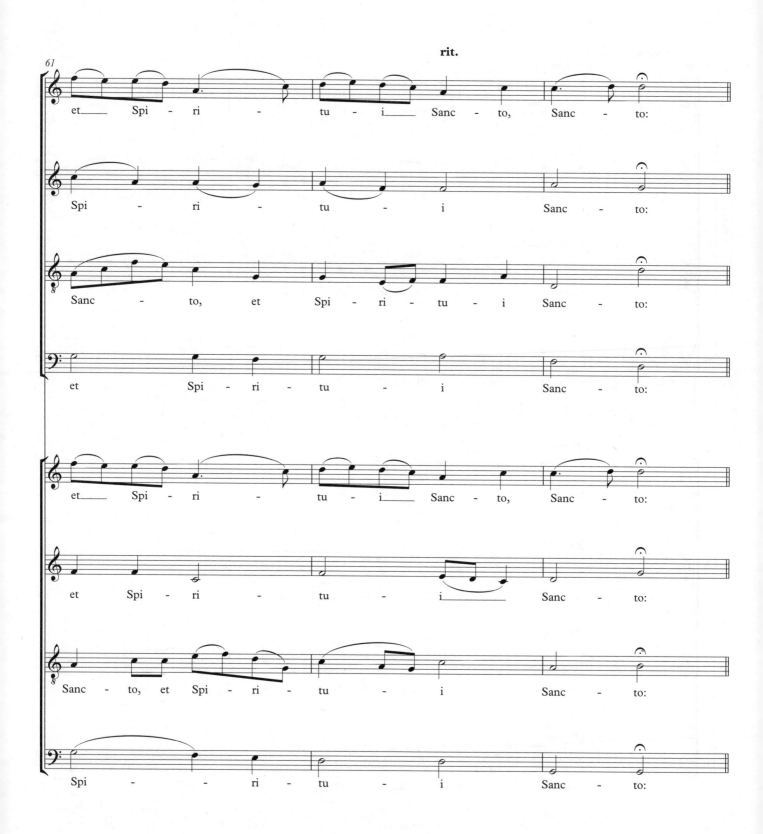

et___ Spi - ri - tu i___ Sanc - to, Sanc - to:

Spi - ri - tu - i Sanc - to:

Sanc - to, et Spi - ri - tu - i Sanc - to:

et Spi - ri - tu - i Sanc - to:

et___ Spi - ri - tu - i___ Sanc - to, Sanc - to:

et Spi - ri - tu - i___ Sanc - to:

Sanc - to, et Spi - ri - tu - i Sanc - to:

Spi - - ri - tu - i Sanc - to:

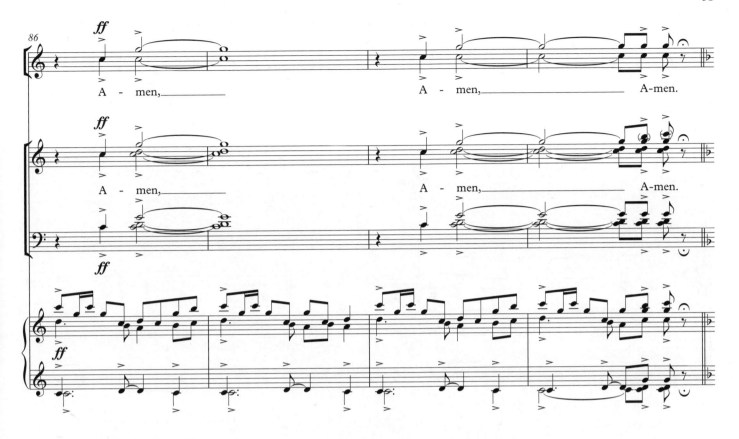

5. Motet: When to the temple Mary went

Johannes Eccard (1553–1611)
trans. Revd John Troutbeck (1832–99)

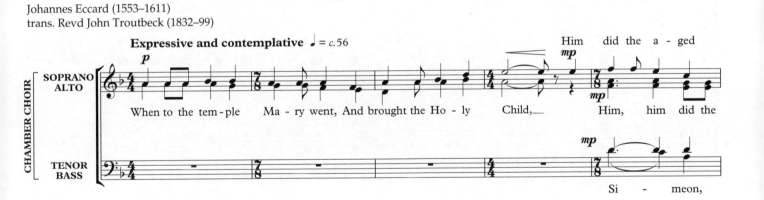

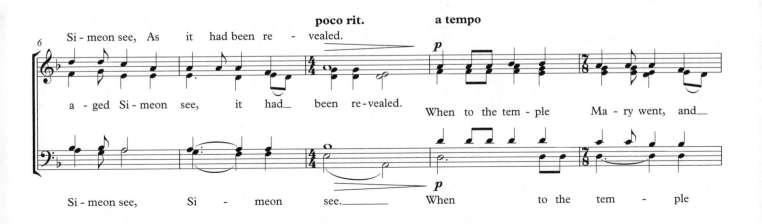

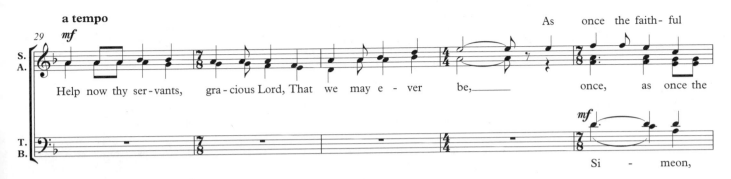

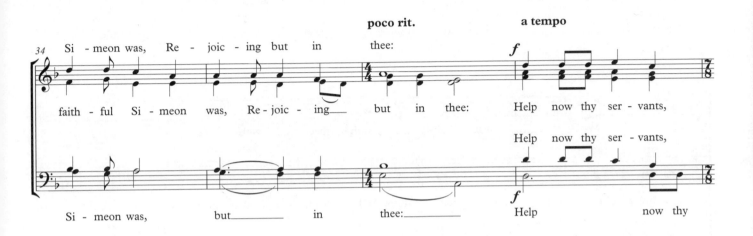

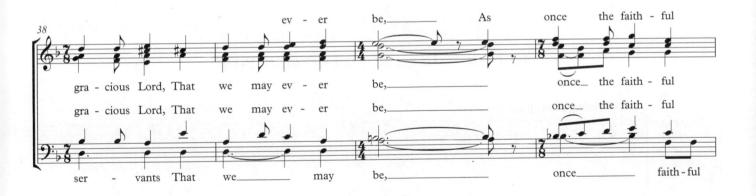

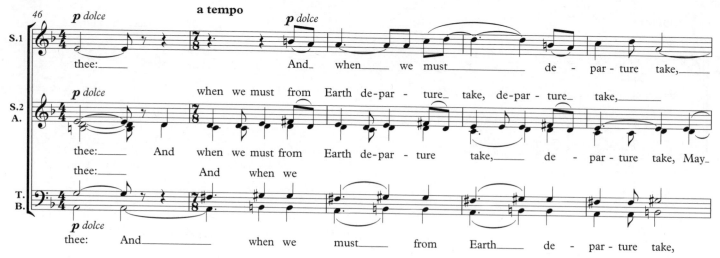

6. Psalm 121 (122): Laetatus sum

40

rit.

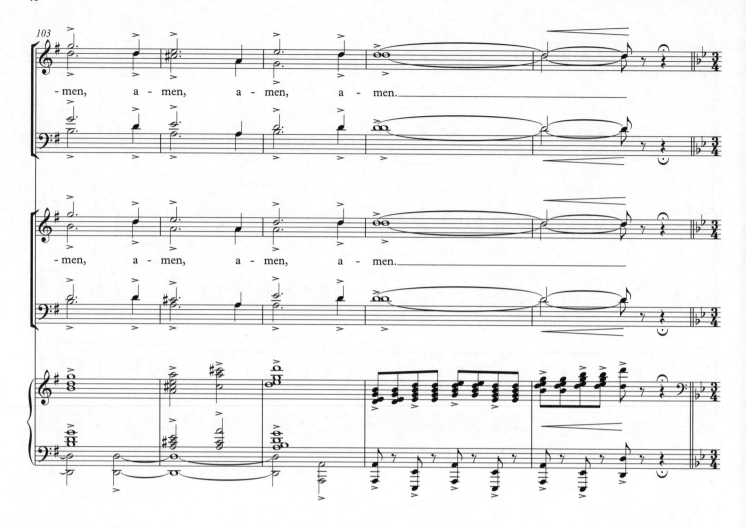

103

- men, a - men, a - men, a - men._____

- men, a - men, a - men, a - men._____

7. Motet: *Lovely tear of lovely eye*

Anon. 14th century

With stillness (Tempo I) ♩ = *c.*54

p espress.

Love-ly tear of love-ly eye,____ Why dost thou me so woe?____

p espress.

SOPRANO
ALTO

TENOR
BASS

CHAMBER CHOIR

With stillness (Tempo I) ♩ = *c.*54

(Perc.)

PIANO

p

p

Sor-row-ful tear of sor-row-ful eye, Thou break-est my heart in two.

Poco più mosso (Tempo II) ♩ = c.60

Thou griev-est sore, Thy sor-row is more Than man-kind's mouth may tell;

Thou singst of sor-row, Man-kind to bor-row, Out of the pit of

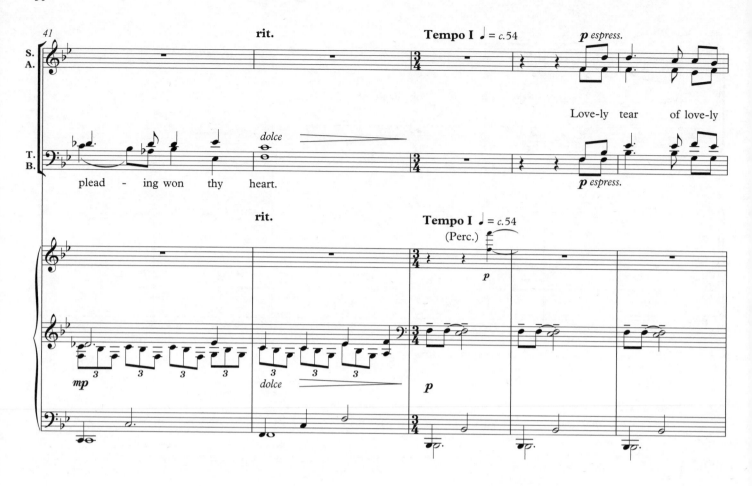

eye,_____ Thou break - est my heart in two._____

eye,_____ Thou break - est my heart in two._____

Tempo II ♩ = *c.*60

Thy heart is rent, Thy bo - dy bent U-pon the rood_____ tree;_____ The

wea-ther is passed, The de - vil de-feat - ed, rit.

wea - ther is passed,__ The de - vil de-feat - ed, Christ, through the might of__ thee.___

might of thee.___

rit.

mf espress.

Tempo I ♩ = c.54

p espress.

Love-ly tear of love - ly eye,___ Why_ dost thou me so

p espress.

Tempo I ♩ = c.54

p

mp espress.

p

8. Hymn: Vexilla Regis prodeunt

Venantius Fortunatus (530–609)

58

Sal - ve, sal - ve, sal-ve, a - ra,

Sal-ve, a - ra, sal-ve, vic - ti - ma, de pas-si-o-nis glo-ri - a, qua

sal - ve, sal - ve, vic - ti - ma.

vi - ta mor-tem per-tu-lit et mor-te vi-tam red-di - dit.

O crux a - ve, spes u - ni - ca, hoc Pas-sio - nis

*Bars 91–9 may also be sung by the congregation.

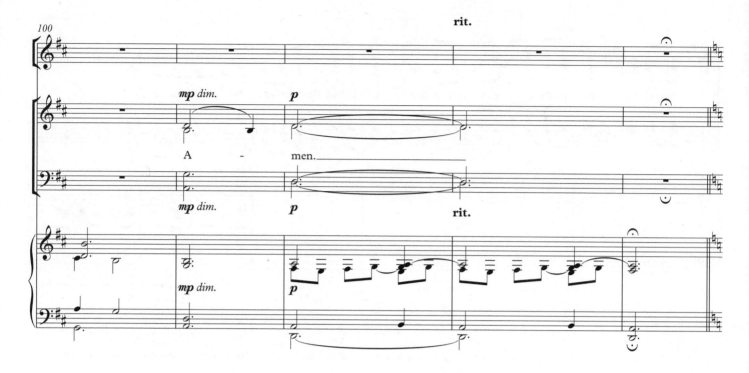

9. Motet: Hail, Star of the sea most radiant

Sarum Primer, 1516

*This part may be sung by a few sopranos and altos from either the chamber choir (preferable) or the children's choir.

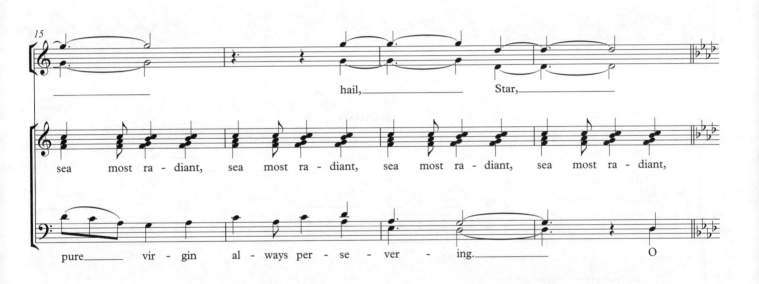

64

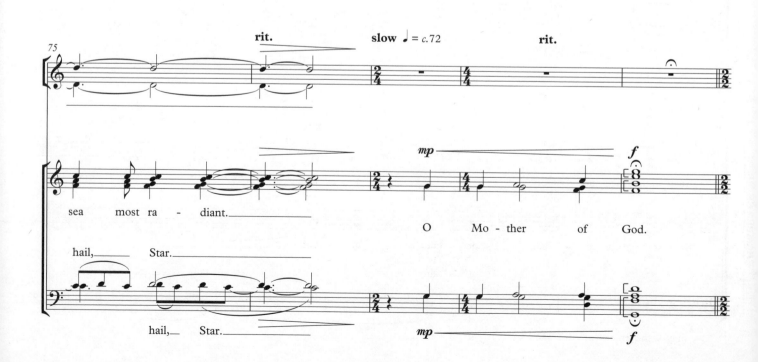

10. Magnificat

1. Magnificat anima mea

Luke 1: 46–55

*The children's choir should join choir 2 (soprano and alto lines).

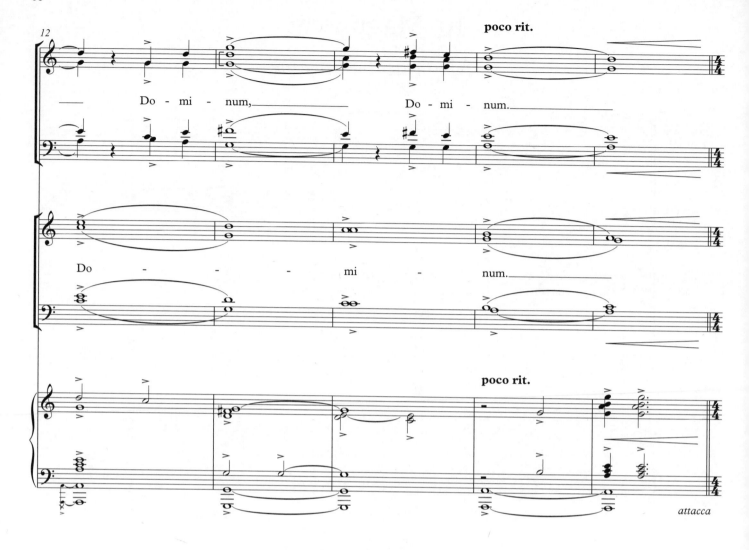

2. Et exultavit

3. Quia respexit

4. Quia fecit mihi magna

5. Et misericordia

6. Fecit potentiam

7. Deposuit potentes de sede

et ex - al - ta - vit

hu - - mi - les.

hu - mi - les, hu - mi - les.

8. Esurientes implevit bonis

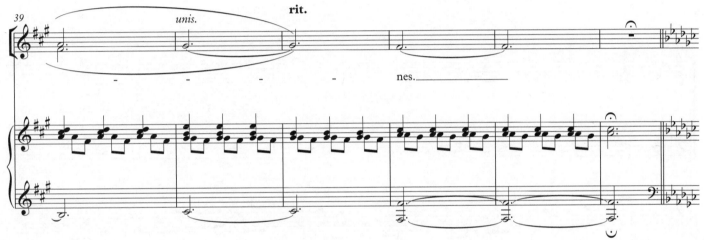

9. Suscepit Israel

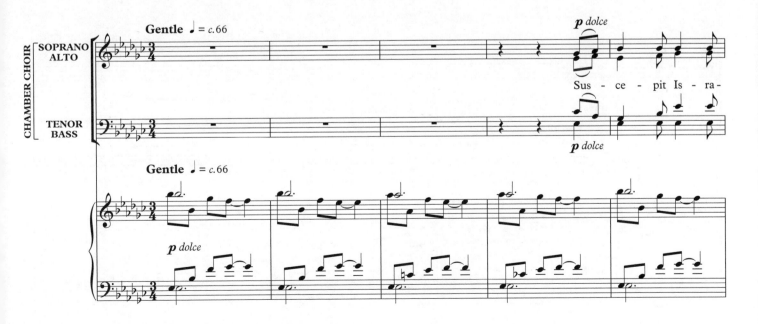

-el, sus - ce - pit___ pu - e - rum su -

-um: re - cor-da - tus

mi-se - ri - cor - di - ae___ su - - -

su - - ae,

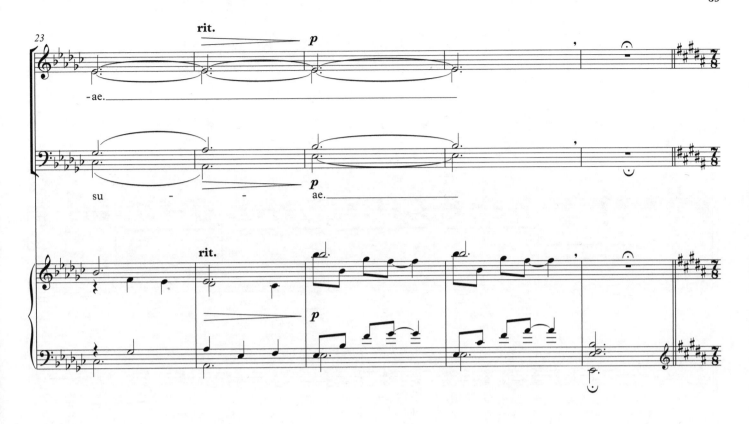

10. Sicut locutus est

est _____ ad pa - tres nos - tros, ad pa - tres nos - tros: _____

-cut lo-cu-tus est ad pa-tres nos - tros, ad pa-tres nos - tros: _____

ff

A - bra-ham et se - mi - ni e - ius in sae -

ff

ff

1.   2.

- cu - la. _____

fff

11. Gloria Patri

12. Sicut erat in principio

nunc et sem - - per,_____

et in sae-cu - la sae-cu-lo - - rum. A -

- men,_____ A - men,_____

Processed in England by Enigma Music Production Services, Amersham, Bucks.
Printed in England by Halstan & Co. Ltd., Amersham, Bucks.